Fluffly Finds his Well-being

Creator and illustrator: Patrick Arguin

English translation: Bleu Dactylo

French version written by: Michèle Rappe
Support, coaching and collaboration: Hélène Beaudette

I want to offer my deepest gratitude to Hélène Beaudette.
Her unconditional support and presence allowed TOOLS OF THE HEART to grow and come into form.

In the garden, the air is cooling with each day that passes, and most of the leaves on the trees have turned from green to yellow, red and orange. Autumn is undoubtedly here!

For the past few days now, Fluffy has been very busy preparing food reserves for the cold season. But this afternoon, the squirrel is really tired and gets easily upset. His stacks of acorns keep tumbling down, and he has to keep starting over.

Colin notices Fluffy's agitation and proposes that he gets some rest to calm down. But Fluffy is stubborn, and he suddenly swings at the acorns and shouts.

«I will never make it!»

The squirrel is red with anger and feels like crying. He stops his work and climbs up into the oak, and looks down at the scattered acorns.

«My heart is beating so fast it feels like it is about to explode!» thinks Fluffy while feeling his heartbeat in his chest.

Fluffy takes deep breaths.
He inhales deeply and exhales slowly.

He feels his heartbeat getting slower,
and his agitation settling down.

White, the elf, appears and calmly starts talking to the squirrel. «Hello Fluffy! Did you notice that by breathing in slowly and putting your paws on your heart, you discovered something important?»

Fluffy is not sure that he understands.

«Remember how you felt before climbing up the tree?» says the elf.

The squirrel recalls his agitation and how being angry felt so unpleasant and uncomfortable.

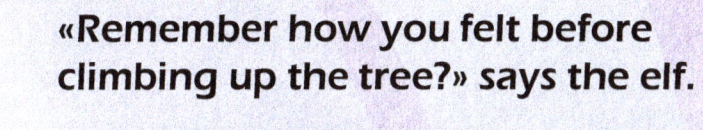

«By taking care of yourself and by giving yourself a hug, you have calmed the beatings of your heart, and you gradually felt well again.»

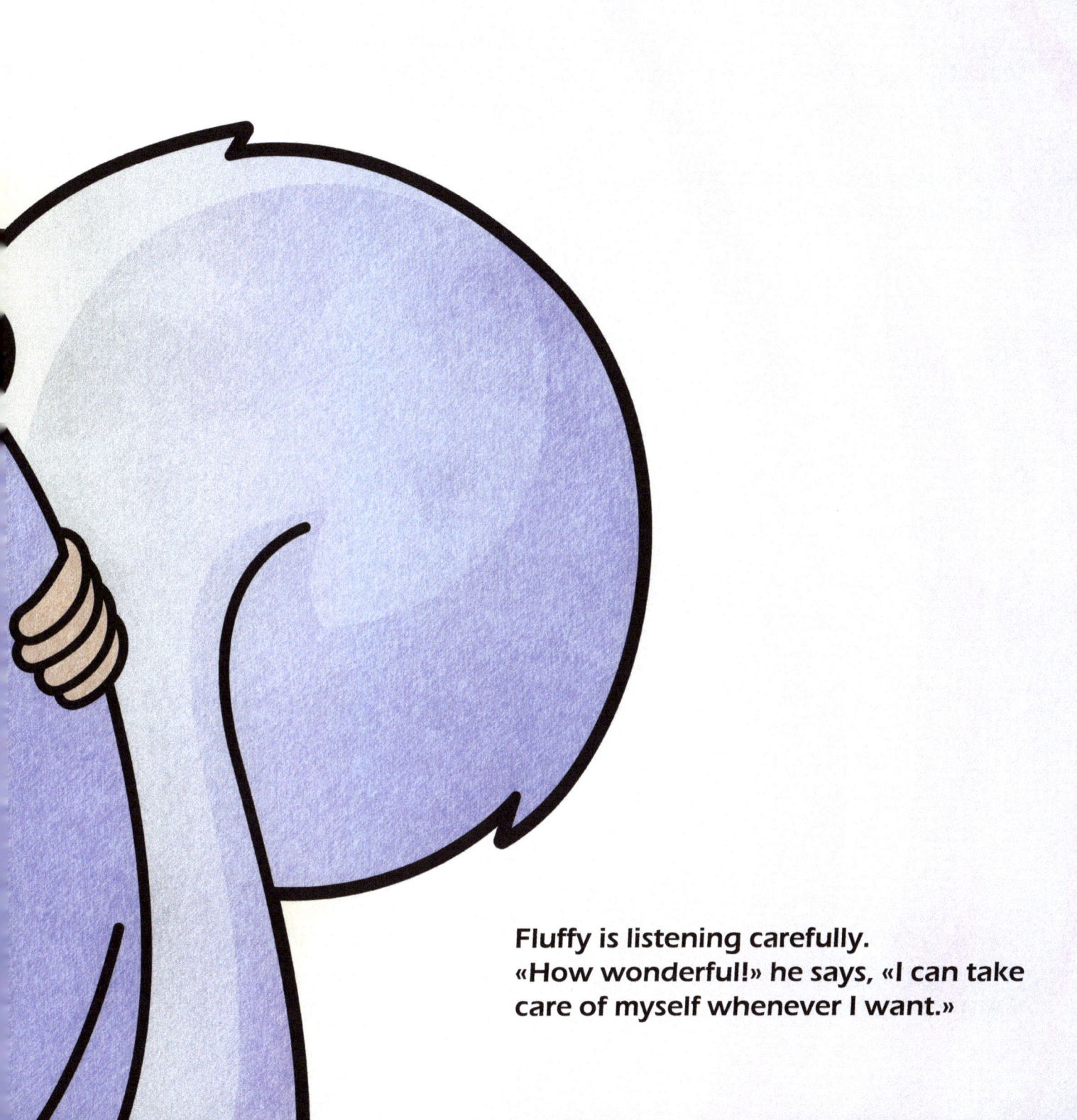

Fluffy is listening carefully.
«How wonderful!» he says, «I can take care of myself whenever I want.»

«Yes!» says White. «And by doing so, you can reconnect with your joy, your well-being and even, new ideas!»

Fluffy is well and feels a calm inside; as if everything was illuminated around him.

«Always remember the treasure inside your heart and all the beautiful qualities and talents that make you who you are!» White says before leaving.

The squirrel opens his eyes and smiles at Father Sun.
«I'm ready to work again!» he decides.
«Oh! And I can build a sled to transport my acorns!»

«Colin! Colin! I feel calm again, and I have something
really wonderful to tell you,» joyfully shouts Fluffy.

«When you don't feel well,» he says with enthusiasm, «you can take care of yourself by taking deep breaths and putting your paws on your heart.»
«But I have no paws!» says Colin laughing.

Fluffy looks at his friend with sadness.
«Do not worry,» says Colin.
«I can also breathe deeply and take care of
myself from my roots to the tip of my leaves.»

«Hello, dear friends!» sings Hazel.
«What are you up to?»

Fluffy tells her what just happened.
Hazel offers to help him with his acorns.

While Father Sun slowly sets, Colin takes
a moment to visit his inner garden and
find his rainbow of wisdom. Every day,
he finds time to take care of himself.

That night under the bright stars, Hazel, Colin and Fluffy talked for a long time about ways to take care of themselves and visit their inner garden.

The stars in the sky created a sparkling cover; slowly everyone closed their eyes. This time, to visit the land of dreams.

A few weeks have passed.

Father Sun and Mother Earth are proud of their peaceful garden.

They know it will continue to flourish, and that each heart holds a wonderful treasure: LOVE.

Remember...

What can I do when I am angry and want to scream and shout?

By putting your hands on your heart and breathing deeply, you will feel the calm slowly settling in. When the calm is there, the anger goes away like a cloud blown by the wind.

What can I do if I am alone and need a hug?

If no one is around to hold and hug you, you can put your hands on yourself and think about love. It can also help you when you feel pain somewhere or get hurt.

What can I do if I forget about the tools or how to use them?

By rereading the stories, you will remember all these useful tools, and it will help you to know how and when to use them.

The Book Collection

Tools of the Heart
Fostering Confidence and Self-esteem

1 Father Sun and Mother Earth Create Life
Breathing/Finding your rhythm

Breathing is essential to life; conscious breathing is a simple, yet effective way to regain your calm and well-being by finding your body's rhythm.

2 Fluffy and the Rainbow in his Heart
Meditation/Finding your inner calm

Each one of us has a peaceful place inside their heart. Meditation is a tool that allows you to find your personal space or to go back to it.

3 Colin Discovers Confidence
Grounding/Strengthening your self-confidence

Growing up often comes with its share of fears and hesitations. Growing solid roots helps to build and nurture a positive self-confidence.

4 Colin and Fluffy Become Friends
Knowing yourself/Loving and appreciating

Positive self-confidence and self-esteem are the building blocks of healthy relationships; therefore, learning to appreciate who we are is a treasure for life.

5 The Choice
Insight/Listening to your intuition

Learning to listen to your inner voice and how to trust it, is learning to stay true to yourself in all situations.

6 Colin's Courage
Expressing/Confidence in yourself

Standing up for yourself is not wrong. It is about relying on your self-worth with confidence, to respectfully say what you need to say.

7 Enough is Enough
Self-respect/Daring to be yourself

Developing good communication skills also implies expressing your feelings and needs in a respectful manner, which can sometimes be a challenge!

8 Fluffy Finds his Well-being
Self-awareness/Taking responsibility

Growing up is also about becoming more aware of your emotions and learning to manage them responsibly.

The Meditation Collection

Tools of the Heart
Fostering Confidence and Self-esteem

Specially designed for young children, the guided meditations explore and develop the same themes, as seen in the **Tools of the Heart** book collection. These intend to reinforce the children's knowledge of themselves through their inner space of wisdom, where things can be seen, heard, and felt.

Meditation is also a wonderful tool that children can easily learn to help them self-regulate physically, mentally, and emotionally.

To learn more, go to our website:
www.toolsoftheheart.com